Margherita Asso

naples
the sunshine city
and its bay

80 Colour Plates

Misenum. Sunset

Pompeii

THE CITY OF NAPLES

Naples, as seen today, is a city full of surprises and disorientation for the tourist arriving for the first time. It is impossible to understand its character and peculiar aspects during a rapid tour. Its structure is complex and disorderly, the monuments appear in such contrast with the urban scene, the aspects of the natural landscape surrounding the city present such variety; furthermore, the people and their way of life are so extraordinary. Yet the character of the city, its particular mode of living, are the direct result of these very contrasts; a character that, while complex and disorderly, is never dull.

The Landscape: Let us imagine how this stretch of land must have appeared in remotest antiquity when its first inhabitants came and settled. A deep inlet lapped by the waters of a sea rarely moved by storms, because it was protected by the long arms of the Sorrento Peninsula and Cape Miseno. Along the coast a chain of hills revealed through their vegetation the tufaceous structure of a terrain opening into hollows and caves. In this natural configuration, sometimes pastoral, sometimes harsh, all the tones of green were in perpetual contrast with the rich yellow tufa with its warm golden tint. And it was this stone, used subsequently as construction material, which determined the characteristic colour of the city. Above this peaceful smiling scene towered Vesuvius. Such a landscape, together with a particular climate, not only influenced the city and conditioned its development, but also determined the character of the people. Natural caves on the sides of the hills offered comfortable refuge. Abundant means of subsistence existed in the particularly fertile land and in the sea, always calm and rich in fish. **The climate** was mild in every season so that life and work could be carried on in the open air. There were no problems of how to combat a hostile Nature. Thus, life must have seemed easy to the first inhabitants of the gulf. It was possible to conduct commercial exchanges and all kinds of encounters and negotiations with nearby peoples. These were characterized by reciprocal trust and tranquil equilibrium. Such peaceable relations brought with them the abolition of all material and moral barriers between man and man, population and population. So the character of this people was formed by the natural setting even before the city rose. Even today we find this character in the streets of Naples, most of all in the old quarter where everyone lives and works in a community, each participating in the life of others. On their thresholds, carpenter, fruiterer, bookseller and vendor of fried foods manage to attend to their work without losing sight of the life going on beyond their doorways. They display their wares on the streets in the most ingenious manner. Every architectural element which might lend itself to better display is exploited, even the steps and balustrades of nearby churches. Among their activities is included discussions with neighbouring shopkeepers, with passers-by and with the chance, probably unknown, customer who has stopped for a chat. The « b a s s i » offer another example of this particular way of life and of this concept of human relations. These are characteristic ground floor dwellings that open directly on to the street with a single door

Naples, Castel Nuovo. Triumphal Arch

Naples, The Gaiola. A tufaceous wall

and window combined. Generally the space inside is insufficient for the needs of a family. They all go out into the street for any activity. Here children play, elderly folk sit in groups gossiping among themselves, the women perform domestic tasks and discuss the latest news of the area. But even if the dwelling were spacious and comfortable, the Neapolitan just could not live without that human contact which lures him out into the street to blend his private life with that of others, to organize his small community like a tribal group where joys and sorrows, festivities and misfortunes, are shared in common. So the grief of one family becomes a grief for the entire community and the rejoicing of one means rejoicing for all. This manner of living, pregnant with human significance, enriches the individual's power of comprehension, his sensitivity and his humanity. This, therefore, helps to make the Neapolitans spiritually among the richest people of this earth. They are always ready to share their wealth provided there are those who wish to receive. Just as when the world was still young, the nature of the region gave generously of its riches to the dwellers in the bay: its sun, the fruits of earth and sea; and just as the landscape was a determining factor in forming the inhabitants'

Naples. Forcella

character, so too did the Neapolitans create their city giving it a form and life perfectly in harmony with their nature. In other words, the Neapolitan needed a particular setting for the way of life that is his and so he created it. In the same way a troupe of strolling players can create their setting, arranging the wings, backgrounds and scenery with imagination and fantasy, taste and spontaneity. **The street** is the stage for improvisation. It is the background of daily life, traditional festivals, great processions, illuminations and fireworks. Narrow dark streets where the only natural element of a famous landscape is a strip of sky peeping out between the cornices of the tall buildings; where the walls break suddenly into great doorways giving one a glimpse of an airy courtyard and the scenic background of an open staircase or a loggia. Luminous streets midway up the hill or along the sea-shore, closed towards the hill by a never-ending succession of houses, opening at their lower levels to vast panoramas. Silent and tranquil stepped streets ascend the hill in ramps and hairpin bends. At every turn they reveal surprising glimpses of a still intact natural environment, flowery terraces and cupolas glistening with colourful majolicas. For the rest, the suggestion of theatrical scenario in the streets of Naples

is not just accidental: every Neapolitan has the feeling and inclination for theatrical representation. The spontaneity and naturalness of ordinary life do not detract from his awareness that every day he is an actor on a stage and has a precise part in the play. Theatrical in manner are the **traditional festivals,** such as that of the Carmine on July 16th, with a spectacular blaze from the belfry of the Carmine as its finale; or that of Piedigrotta, on September 8th at the Villa Comunale, backed by public illuminations of genuine virtuosity. Theatrical are the great processions and religious feasts such as that of San Gennaro on September 19th, when all Naples pours into the Cathedral and its adjacent streets. The crowd itself becomes spectator and chief actor in the special ceremony during which the phases of the miracle of San Gennaro are eagerly watched. Theatrical are the churches decorated in a profusion of velvet, silk, ribbons, carpets and flowers. For such decorations one calls on the skill of the specialized « addobbatore », one of the most flourishing tradesmen of this city. So too, at some important funerals, one even finds a sumptuous hearse drawn by four pairs of horses: mighty creatures which recall the horses painted by Piero della Francesca. Even the Neapolitan crib is a form of

Naples, S. Maria del Carmine. Festival of the Carmine. Blaze on belfry tower

theatre. From its rudimentary inceptions, thanks to the work of noted artists in the 18th century, it rose to the level of true artistic expression. On the subject of the crib, it is worth while emphasizing that the principal scene is never the Nativity. The Neapolitan **presepio** is the representation of the day-to-day life of the people in a natural and urban setting. No detail is lacking which forms part of the Naples of yesterday, today and ever: from the solitary ruins of a classical temple to the tavern with hams and cheeses hanging from the beams; from the hills of golden tufa clad in Mediterranean vegetation to the houses with their flower-covered terraces. In this setting the crowd is the true and only protagonist. It is the most heterogeneous that can be imagined: from the poultry seller just arrived from the country, to the rich merchants who come from across the seas; from the strolling minstrels, to the plebeian woman with her shopping bag; from the host serving macaroni at table before the door of his tavern, to the sly cheating Moor. Although today there are no 18th century gold-embroidered silk garments, we still encounter the same crowd, the same types and characters in the streets of Old Naples.

Caserta, Royal Palace.
The Crib (Detail)

Caserta, Royal Palace. The Crib (Figures)

8

NAPLES THROUGH THE CENTURIES

The boundaries of the city **Neapolis** are well-known and precise. It was founded in the sixth century B. C. by Greek colonists coming from Cumae on the north coast of the Gulf, which had already been populated for centuries by villages and Greek colonies. It was bounded by the present day Via Foria and Via S. Maria di Costantinopoli, Corso Umberto I and Via Colletta. Neapolis was divided according to the chessboard scheme conceived by Hippodamus of Miletus; three d e c u m a n i were intersected by c a r d i n e s. The outlines of these are to be found intact even today (the decumanus was a street going from East to West, the cardo from North to South). Founded by a highly civilized people, favoured by the mildness of the climate and the richness of the soil, the city flourished splendidly during a long period of prosperity and independence. Neapolis succeeded in maintaining its autonomy after Rome appeared on the shores of the bay, desirous of acquiring the city as an ally and of cutting it off from the infiltrations of the Samnites. It remained a faithful ally of Rome in the struggles against Pyrrhus and Hannibal. Even after it had been degraded to the level of a municipium by the effects of the L e x J u l i a, Neapolis preserved the Greek language and institutions. This was a thing not merely tolerated, but in a certain sense encouraged by the Romans themselves. They were notoriously fascinated by Greek culture and found in the nearby city the ideal spot for study and pleasure, for shorter and longer sojourns. The sumptuous villas which flourished along the coast from Baiae to Posillipo, at Pizzofalcone, at Herculaneum, at Capri and Ischia, bear witness to the interest which the Romans had in this land. The remains of these villas which have come down to us, together with an entire literature of the epoch, provide us with an insight into an extremely refined and cultured «sct» of patrons and artists, poets and literary figures. As has been

Naples, Church of S. Gregorio Maggiore. Apse

said, the street layout of the Greek city still remains today in its entire nucleus. The constructions remain incorporated in the buildings erected above them in a continuous and constant stratification over succeeding centuries. The catacombs of San Gennaro, together with

Naples, National Museum. Venus with Cupids (Marble statue, copy of that by Dedalsa of Bithynia)

Naples, Cathedral. Baptistry, Mosaics

an entire series of catacombs still only partly explored, bear witness to early Christianity at Naples. They also offer great interest from the artistic point of view on account of the frescoes which they preserve, and also for the spatial organization of certain sections. The fall of the empire was followed by a short period of ups and downs. Naples was several times captured by the Goths and then lost again to the Byzantines. The latter finally entered into definitive possession of the city in the middle of the 6th century. The new influx of Byzantine peoples revived and renewed in the ancient Greek city the tradition and culture which linked it to the East, and its mother-country Greece. But there are extremely few artistic evidences of this period, which, nevertheless must have been very rich for the city in architectural developments as well. A recall to this past is seen in the **mosaic decoration** of the Baptistery and in the apses of S. Giovanni Maggiore and S. Giorgio Maggiore.

But new times were approaching for the city. Despite the struggle against the Longobards it gradually freed itself from the domination of Byzantium. Among the people the gradual transformation of the internal political order coincided with the re-awakening of a feeling of autonomy and in a renewed

Naples, Church of S. Chiara, Cloister of the Grey Friars and side of Church

military awareness. The politics of Pope Gregory I were also involved. At the end of the 6th century he aided the Neapolitans in a crucial moment of their struggle against the Longobards. Apart from this, Byzantium, perturbed by the expansion of Longobard power in southern Italy, encouraged the development of autonomy and a military state in Naples in order to counterbalance the menace. We are in the year 661: the emperor Constans II names the first duke: **the duchy of Naples** has its beginnings. A century later, subsequent to other events, it is to acquire complete independence from Byzantium. Through the political acumen of its dukes and the military valour of its entire population, it will succeed in preserving this independence until the middle of the 12th century. For four centuries Naples is enriched in art and culture, and is enlarged, even beyond the city walls, with new buildings. There were two cathedrals, numerous churches and convents, four major basilicas. Studies were promoted, a library founded in the bishop's palace, the Dukes' Palace was constructed. To the old naval harbour a second had to be added in order to handle the traffic of the merchant marine occupied in a dense network of trade with the East. Halfway through the 12th century, however, the duchy could no longer

Naples, Capodimonte,
National Gallery. Simone Martini:
S. Ludovico of Toulouse crowns
his brother, Robert of Anjou,
King of Naples

resist the power of the Normans, who had already taken over all of southern Italy. The **Norman-Swabian domination** (1140—1266) was an unfortunate interval in the history of Naples, above all because once the autonomy of preceding centuries was suffocated, every hope of development towards a free commune was extinguished. In the field of art, too, Naples assumed a second-rate position in comparison with Palermo, which had been chosen as capital of the kingdom. On the other hand the Neapolitans failed to recognize the new political spirit of Frederick II of Swabia and the advantages which might have accrued to the city from the founding of the University in 1224. The advent of the **Angevin dynasty** (1226) brought Naples' re-acquisition of its role as capital of the kingdom. The aim of the Angevins was to create a great power in the West. The awakening of the city was total: commercial relations intensified, particularly with France, Florence and Genoa; the number of merchants' «lodges» increased; the University drew professors and students from all parts of Italy; literary figures, poets and philosophers, such as Boccaccio, Petrarch and Thomas Aquinas, gravitated towards Naples. Contemporaneously the Angevins undertook a program of architectural and artistic renewal, inviting French

Naples. Castle of S. Elmo

Naples, S. Martino, National Museum. The «Tavola Strozzi» (by unknown designer, XV cent.)

Naples. Aragonese tower

architects and Tuscan artists to Naples. The absence of a local culture
capable of interpreting in its own manner the architecture from beyond the
Alps, brought about the acceptance of the forms and traditions of the
French Gothic. Today it is to be seen in the churches of S. Chiara, S. Eli-
gio, Donnaregina, and in the apse of S. Lorenzo Maggiore. Nothing remains
of the civil buildings of the era. Castel Nuovo, the Angevin palace constructed by the French architects Pierre d'Agincourt and Pierre de Chaul,
was transformed in the next century. Among the figurative artists who
worked at the Angevin court, Giotto, Simone Martini, Pietro Cavallini, Tino
di Camaino and Lando di Pietro made an imprint which was to remain even
during successive decades. Meanwhile the Sienese style also influenced
contemporary architecture. This is indicated by the architectural character
of the «Chiostro dei Minori» in S. Chiara and the portico of the church of
the «Incoronata». But there was no adequate enlargement of the city cor-
responding to the architectural renewal and many new buildings began to
occupy gardens. Thus began a series of problems which today have reached
macroscopic proportions.

The Aragonese Dynasty, which succeeded that of the Angevins roughly

Naples. View with Via Roma (formerly Via Toledo) on left

midway through the 1500's, confronted the urbanistic problems following a precise program reflecting the spirit of the Renaissance. Eastwards the city was enlarged by the construction of a new peripheral wall, which survives to a great part today. Later this was extended to the north and west over a section later demolished in the enlargement of the 16th century. In the buildings we find side-by-side the work of Tuscan artists, such as Giuliano da Maiano who constructed Porta Capuana, and Spanish architects. The latter bring to Naples the typical forms of Catalan architecture and are exemplified by figures such as Sagrera, creator of the Hall of the Barons in Castel Nuovo. The renewal of Castel Nuovo, which is so minutely represented in the so-called **Tavola Strozzi,** belongs to this period. The view the Tavola offers of the Naples of 1479 is the image of a flourishing city. At the end of the century the kingdom was conquered by Charles VIII of France. After a brief war between France and Spain the latter had the better of a struggle for the possession of southern Italy. Thus begins the long period of **Spanish domination** in Naples accompanied by an entire series of demographic and building problems connected with the sudden and vast immigration into the city of noble families from the kingdom of

19

Naples, Monastery of S. Martino. Cloister (Detail)

Spain, of spanish functionaries and of the military. The vice-roy Pietro di Toledo dealt with the problem by enlarging the city to the west beyond the Aragonese city walls. He simultaneously opened a long wide road which was called after him Via Toledo (the present-day Via Roma). He set up a dense network of streets between this road and the hill of S. Elmo and along these aligned the buildings of the «quartieri». An edict of 1566 prohibited the construction of new houses outside the city walls. In spite of this, the needs of the ever-increasing population were such that vast new suburbs arose beyond the walls. But, as even this was not sufficient, the surviving gardens were destroyed. Buildings were constructed in the city on every open space. Houses rose to such heights that the proportion between buildings and open spaces was wrecked. The small delightful city of the Aragonese period was transformed into an enormous, congested, unhygienic conglomeration of houses and individuals. In 1656 Naples reaped the fruits of this urbanistic policy: a plague broke out reducing the inhabitants from 360,000 to 160,000. A different aspect of the enthusiasm for building in this period was the renewal and construction of many churches and mansions. Among the architects was the figure of Cosimo Fanzago

Naples, Capodimonte. The Royal Palace

whose work played an incisive part in characterizing the Neapolitan architecture of the first half of the 17th century. The enlargement of the Certosa di S. Martino, the renewal of S. Giorgio Maggiore and the Palazzo Donn'Anna represent a few of the numerous works in which Fanzago reveals his links with classical tradition, notwithstanding the taste for richness in decoration, typical of his time. In other fields, Spanish mis-government was shown by the ever-increasing taxes. Discontent arose among the populace and resulted in two revolutions (one of which was that led by Masaniello). In 1734, after a few decades of the Austrian rule which had substituted that of Spain, **Charles of Bourbon** entered Naples. He restored with new capital the autonomous kingdom of old and there began a happier period, full of promise. Charles, guided by the new theories of the philosophic movement of Enlightenment, favoured the middle and lower classes. He began the construction of new buildings: the Albergo dei Poveri (Hostel of the poor), the S. Carlo Theatre, the royal palace of Capodimonte. This palace was to contain the collection of paintings, sculpture and objets d'art which had belonged to the Farnese family, and had come into Charles' possession through his mother Elisabetta Farnese. Included were portraits of members

21

Naples, Capodimonte, National Gallery.
Titian: Pope Paolo III, with nephews
Ottavio and Alessandro Farnese

Naples, Capodimonte, National Gallery.
Andrea Mantegna: Portrait of Francesco
Gonzaga

Naples, Capodimonte, National Gallery.
Pieter Brueghel: The Parable of the Blind
(Tempera)

Naples, National Museum.
Ercole Farnese
(Marble statue 3.17 metres)

of the Farnese family by Titian, works by Sebastiano del Piombo, Parmigianino, Correggio and Mantegna; sculptures of Roman times, mainly found among the ancient ruins in Rome during the pontificate of the Farnese Pope, Paul III. To this period belong the first finds at Pompei and Herculaneum. Vanvitelli and Fuga were the two principal architects of the time and worked on numerous mansions and churches.

In 1759 **Ferdinand IV** succeeded Charles, who had become King of Spain. and continued his father's policy with the aid of Charles's shrewd minister, Tanucci. But it was in the character of the city that the most interesting transformation took place. The small province which had risen to capital status suddenly found itself in contact with different peoples and countries which opened it up to new experiences in culture, new interests and customs. In the 1800's it was imperative for the cultured foreigner to visit Italy, and that included Naples. Some of them ended by residing at length in the city, almost succeeding in becoming Neapolitans. They were attracted by the cosmopolitan life, the interesting encounters Naples offered and the links so easily formed. The Court, the embassies and the cultural institutes attracted artists, literary folk, diplomats, soldiers, archaeologists

Naples, S. Martino, National Museum. Antonio Joli: Departure of King Charles from Naples (1759)

and adventurers. The events of the French Revolution also had repercussions in Naples in the short-lived Parthenopean Republic of 1798—99. In 1805, after the victory of Napoleon over Austria, there began a period of history known as the French decade. This saw the removal of the Bourbons and the installations on the throne of the Two Sicilies firstly of Joseph Bonaparte, subsequently of Gioacchino Murat. The decade brought new works of transformation to Naples, such as the construction of Via Posillipo and the road to Capodimonte, the creation of such institutions as the Botanical Gardens, the Conservatory of Music, the Bank of Naples and the Astronomical Observatory. The Bourbon dynasty was restored after 1815 and Naples, too, took part in the more widespread movements which were preparing for the unification of Italy. There was the construction of the church of S. Francesco di Paola in front of the Royal Palace, of the first Italian railway (Naples - Portici), of the road which winds midway around the hill and was first named after Maria Teresa and subsequently became Corso Vittorio Emanuele; these were the principal works of the last years of the kingdom. In 1860 Garibaldi found in Naples a soil fertile for the annexation to Italy of the kingdom of the Two Sicilies.

Naples, Piazza Plebiscito. Church of S. Francesco di Paola

Naples. San Carlo Theatre

Naples

AN EXCURSION BY THE SEA

For every city which arises beside water, be it sea, river, or lake, there exists a relationship between one and the other, a subtle reciprocal call, a subdued dialogue. It is a particular pleasure to seek this out and find it. Naples is no exception to the rule. In this chapter it is proposed to guide the tourist along

Naples, Marechiaro. Ruins

the coast exploring beaches, tiny harbours, cliffs and rock walls, discovering monuments and the ruins of Roman villas, in an attempt to recognize that subtle call between land and sea, to understand another singular aspect of this city. The excursion begins from the hill of Posillipo and, after some deviations down

the slopes to the shore lying in a natural setting of rich contrasts, will take us to Mergellina and along the sea to Castel dell'Ovo and Castel Nuovo.

On the extreme point of the promontory of Posillipo, on a plateau jutting out over the sea, we find ourselves at the **Belvedere,** an elliptical avenue which wanders around the side of the hill and offers one of the most varied and enchanting views imaginable. The promontory extends between the two bays of Pozzuoli and Naples. To the left we have the arc of the Neapolitan coast. Dotted with houses and overlooked by Vesuvius, it stretches out into the Sorrento Peninsula. Facing us we have the islands of Capri, Ischia and Procida, changing in tints depending on light conditions. To the right lies the promontory of Cape Miseno enclosing the northern side of the gulf. To the right is Pozzuoli. Below is the island of Nisida, connected to the mainland by road. Below the Belvedere, on the side facing Naples, the **hill of Posillipo** descends to the sea. It is covered in rich vegetation in which the green of the pines dominates over that of ilexes, olives and reed thickets. Departing from the Belvedere, we go down Via T. Lucrezio Caro. This street, bordered by two rows of splendid pines, winds in broad curves around the flank of the hill, offering an infinite variety of viewpoints over the bay. Before long a narrow street turns off to the right, going down towards the sea. Now it is banked by walls adorned with a richly varied vegetation, brightened by patches of ever-flowering bouganvillea; now it reveals a view over valleys cultivated with vineyards, over sheer cliffs of yellow tufa on which erosion has embroidered an attractive lacework design. Suddenly it be-

Naples. Marechiaro

comes necessary to proceed on foot: the street becomes narrow and steep descending in steps down to the tiny village of **Gaiola,** a huddle of fishermen's houses. One is aware of the sea nearby, but cannot see where the road will end; enclosed between walls to its last stretch, it keeps to the end one ultimate surprise for the patient leisurely tourist: the discovery of an enchanting inlet. The small beach at the extremely is protected by rocks of yellow tufa; rocks of a softness which has allowed the sea to erode and smooth them, darkening their golden tint, working them into fantastic configurations which are decorated above by patches of prickly pear. Scattered ruins in « o p u s r e t i c u l a t u m » remind us of the Romans' predilection for these places and their sumptuous villas which, going down to the sea, dotted the coastline. On the right of the inlet a few cliffs complete the scene, which gains in fantasy from the names of nearby localities more easily accessible by sea; suggestive names such as Grotta dei Tuoni (Thunder Cave), Cala di Trentaremi (Inlet of Thirty Oars). Turning back by another road (private) one can reach the remains of the Villa Pausilypon, left to Augustus by Vedius Pollio, which gave its name to the hill of Posillipo. The remains of the theatre and

Odéon are worthy of note. Highly reminiscent, too, are the ruins, extending to the shore and, with the passing years, almost blended with the rocks, so that they now seem part of the natural landscape. Returning to Via T. Lucrezio Caro, we continue towards **Marechiaro.** The road descends in a series of curves among villas and vineyards. The small Church of S. Maria del Faro appears in an unusual position, its side facing the street, its Baroque façade greeting those who go down to the sea. Further along the road ends in a group of typical restaurants, and now it is best to proceed on foot, descending a stairway, if one wishes to discover again, at sea level, more cliffs and rocks eroded into evocative forms, fishermen's houses, a few ruins where the prickly pear prevails, even the ruins of a Roman villa. This is called Palazzo dei Spiriti (Mansion of Spirits), from who knows what mysterious echo drawn from its empty arches by the wind and the sea, or maybe from the emotions it arouses in those who manage to visit it. Returning, we realize that the campanile of S. Maria del Faro dominates the entire hamlet whose houses are grouped together with the natural setting in an appealing composition.

Via Posillipo, which we now take in order to descend towards Mergellina,

Naples. S. Maria del Faro

was opened in 1812 during the rule of Gioacchino Murat. The slope to the sea now becomes gentler; a more ordered growth replaces the natural vegetation and the vineyards of the headland. Among the pines and the ilexes there appear other, more valued species, certainly not indigenous. We note the presence of parks, created to enhance elegant villas. Villa Emma, Villa Rosebery, Villa Peirce, Villa Roccaromana and others revived in the last century the ancient tradition of a sojourn on the coast of Posillipo. But in the meantime we have arrived at another fork in the road: to the right it descends to **Cape Posillipo.** We go along it: it is wide and peaceful; the low walls which flanked the little road to Gaiola are here high and almost solemn. They barely succeed in holding back the magnificent parks leaning out over the road. But over the entire hill the walls are built of the characteristic golden tufa which, at some points, rests upon a layer of outcropping rock, following its irregular profile and blending into it. Returning to Via Posillipo and continuing the descent, one reaches the Palazzo di Donn'Anna, which the viceroy Filippo Ramiro Guzman had Fanzago build for his wife in 1642. The Mansion, which was never completed, remains an imposing mass jutting into the water. Here the subdued dia-

Naples. Fisherman

logue between land and sea develops into an elegant conversation. In its finished state there is a rugged beauty which gives it life, like a sculpture roughly outlined in stone. Elegance is added to the view over the sea by a loggia which is repeated on three levels. One can imagine how the Bay of Naples must have been framed by the loggias from within those 17th century halls. Here again the yellow tufa: in the arches, in the 17th century cornices, in the windows with low pediments, in the lesenes which, facing the sea, emphasizes the arches of the loggia. But by now we are at **Mergellina.** At the foot of the hill of Posillipo is a small inlet: a tiny port, fishermen, nets, fish-baskets, sea food, boats and sea air. Wander about for a while amid the confusion and observe what the people do. Talk to the bare-footed «scugnizzi» (urchins) with their sparkling eyes. They certainly will not overlook a tourist from whom they might cadge a coin. Listen to the fishermen talking among themselves in dialect and join in their conversation. Mergellina is a picture of Neapolitan life. A personal discovery of its peculiarities can have the same value as savouring the works of art in the city's most important museum. Now we travel along **Via Caracciolo,** one of the most beautiful streets in the world. Unfortunately

Naples, Posillipo. View of the town

the swift-moving traffic here makes it difficult for us to capture that dialogue between land and sea which was so easy to understand in the unspoiled natural setting we found at the beginning of our excursion. Beyond the stream of traffic, the Villa Comunale is a participant in this dialogue. At least, it was intended so to be, although to-day it is something that seems to have disappeared. The Villa Comunale is a vast public garden, more than a kilometer in length, between Via Caracciolo and the Riviera di Chiaia. Ferdinando IV entrusted its construction to Carlo, son of Luigi Vanvitelli, in 1778. Ilexes, pines, palms, araucarias and eucalyptus frame the sea promenade with their foliage. They lend it that particular amplitude and spaciousness which is its characteristic, while the breakwater reef, ever fringed with white foam, emphasizes the regularity and gentleness of its curve. The Aquarium, established in one of its buildings, possesses a scientific importance which in itself is of great interest, but this apart, it has a special significance when one realises that in it are collected marine specimens found exclusively in the Bay of Naples. The curve of Via Caracciolo comes to an end below the hill of Pizzofalcone, but in the scheme of the landscape should ideally continue to **Castel dell'Ovo,** which we

Naples. Mergellina

have noticed gradually coming nearer. It resembles an abstract sculpture rather than a castle. Its solid walls express a sense of powerful strength, the light and shade of its structure emphasize its plastic beauty. And once again there is the yellow tufa, in the great smooth walls unbroken by apertures, in the sharp corners, in the straight cut embrasures and in the foundations of solid rock with which the walls have merged during the centuries. The reef was called the Island of Megaris and formed part of the Mt. Echia complex where stood the sumptuous villa of Lucullus. Odoacer later banished the emperor Romulus Augustulus to this spot. Here he died in A. D. 476, thereby putting an end to the Roman Empire in the West. In the 6th century Basilian monks instituted a monastery here and also constructed a church dedicated to the Saviour. By mid-12th century, when the Normans took over the city, the monks had already abandoned the island for a considerable time. The Normans realized the suitability of the island for defence purposes and turned it into a fortress as a stronghold for the city. On the southernmost point towards the open sea they constructed a mighty tower called the Torre Normandia. From now on, the island, once a castle, would function as a stronghold. The works of

Naples. Via Caracciolo

fortification to be realized in succeeding centuries are also related to the development of military science. Thus each is superimposed upon, and modifies its predecessor; so too the shape and outline of the castle undergoes progressive changes. In this respect it is interesting to observe from the Tavola Strozzi what the castle looked like in the latter part of the 15th century. In this painting Castel dell'Ovo appears on the extreme left and the buildings are supported by a great arch of stonework.

Now we enter the castle. Ascending a long ramp one passes through a vestibule from which begins the road that crosses the island lengthwise. At some points spaces open towards the sea, so that one has the impression of being in a small ancient hamlet rather than in a fortress. The Byzantine church of the Salvatore (Saviour); the hall of columns, which seems possibly connected with the Roman period of the complex when the villa of Lucullus stood here; the 14th century style loggia with its fine 14 cent. Gothic arches in peperino, designed for assemblies of the court: these are the elements which confer most fascination and interest to the monument. The road terminates at a high point, on a terrace from which there is a splendid view of the city. The tiny port of **S. Lucia** between

Naples. Castel dell'Ovo

the castle and the mainland, and the **Borgo Marinaro** add to the attractive scene a vigorous note of life and colour. Again we take the sea road. After passing a 17th century fountain, the Immacolatella by Pietro Bernini, one descends towards Via Acton.

Castel Nuovo was erected by Charles I of Anjou between 1279 and 1282 as seat of the Angevin court, but was demolished in the war between the Angevins and the Aragonese. It was rebuilt by Ferdinand I of Aragon in 1442. Massive walls and menacing towers in grey peperino create a contrast to the graceful triumphal arch and the elegant exploitation of spaces in the Hall of the Barons. One notices immediately the relation it bears both to the open space facing the sea and to the city above. The mass towers over and imposes itself upon the design of the Renaissance city. It embodies and expresses a precise political idea; that of the prince, of the absolute lord of the Italian Renaissance, To-day, suffocated by modern traffic which pathetic little gardens attempt to keep at a distance, Castel Nuovo only barely conveys that old-time idea, but its gigantic mass still fascinates us, as does its past significance, the history it contains and its dual role of fortress and royal palace. Now we are approaching the trium-

Naples. Immacolatella

Naples. Castel Nuovo

phal arch. It was constructed in 1454 in honour of the triumph of Alfonso I.
Various artists worked on the sculptures, among them certainly Sagrera,
Domenico Gagini, Francesco Laurana and Isaia da Pisa.
The whole has been happily assembled in a general unified design, the
work of an artist still unknown to the critics. Whoever he was, he must
certainly have seen the splendid Porta di Capua which Frederick II of
Swabia had had constructed two centuries before; at Capua, on the
Roman bridge across the Volturno, it was destroyed in the middle of the
16th century. There is an architectural similarity between the arch of
Alfonso of Aragon and the Porta di Capua, the latter also a triumphal arch
in white marble between two towers of grey peperino. This similarity is
not so absurd when one remembers that the arch of Capua dated from that
artistic renewal inspired by Frederick II, which many have seen as a 13th
century Renaissance «ante litteram». Inside the castle we shall be able
to see the splendid bronze door by Guglielmo Monaco da Parigi (1462).
Originally it closed the entrance portal of the castle. It depicts episodes
in the struggle of Ferdinand I against the barons of the Angevin party.
One might also visit the Palatine Chapel, dedicated to S. Barbara. It is the

only part of the Angevin structure which preserves in the splayed window recesses fragments of paintings by Giotto. The hall of the Barons, which has a most interesting octagonal ribbed vault, is the work of G. Sagrera. Beyond the vestibule opens the huge square courtyard, on which looks the Palatine Chapel, called St. Barbara, the only part remaining of the Angevin building. An elegant Renaissance portal in the façade has a statue of the Madonna by Francesco Laurana in the niche above. Inside one observes the remains of paintings by Giotto in the splays of the windows. To the left of the Church, up a XV cent. stairway, is the Hall of the Barons where, during a meal, King Ferrante had arrested all the barons faithful to the Angevin party who had plotted against him. The architecture of this hall is by Guglielmo Sagrera, a Catalan architect; the ribbed vault on an octagonal plan, recalls, by means of small cross-vaults, the square plan of the hall, with a bold play of structures and a spatial effect of great elegance. From the windows the view embraces the Bay. Beneath Castel Nuovo the port is even to-day full of life, of commerce, comings and goings; the **Molo Angioino,** transformed and incorporated by now in the new port arrangements, has preserved its old name.

Naples, Castel Nuovo. Hall of the Barons, Vault

Naples, National Museum.
Victory (Marble statue)

THE ANCIENT CENTRE

If we observe a plan of the city of Naples, we can immediately make out the nucleus of the Greek city, set like a gem in a vast disordered network. Its layout, characterized by three decumani intersected by numerous cardines, appears clear even today after approximately 25 centuries; a proof of the urbanistic value of the small city. The three decumani are Via S. Biagio dei Librai - Vicaria Vecchia, Via Tribunali, Via Sapienza - Anticaglia - Santi Apostoli. But even if the Greek road network has survived intact, not so the buildings, which have been destroyed or incorporated in successive structures during the transformations of centuries. However, sufficient elements remain to reconstruct in our minds the form of the ancient city. The temple of Ceres and that of Apollo rose in the places where now stand the churches of S. Gregorio Armeno and S. Restituta. We find traces of the Odéon and the Greek Theatre in Via Anticaglia and in the same road section in the curve of some alleys behind S. Paolo Maggiore. But the centre of the city was the agora, the forum of Roman times, situated halfway along the decumanus maximus (Via Tribunali). The more important buildings faced this space which has, in time, grown smaller. It was the centre of political, religious and commercial life: here were the Basilica and the Curia, where now stands the church of S. Lorenzo Maggiore; the Temple of the Dioscuri, now the church of S. Paolo Maggiore; the Aerarium (treasury) and the prison, in the area of the present-day church of the Gerolomini; the arcades and the shops. With the passing of centuries all these were incorporated in the buildings which gradually replaced them. Some were destroyed and their most important structural elements utilized in new buildings; e. g. the pillars of the temple of Antinous, now in the apse of S. Giovanni Maggiore. Others became interred or enclosed in successive buildings as the level of the streets was raised. It can be said that every epoch of history has partly cancelled its predecessors and left its own mark. Consequently the ancient centre of Naples is a veritable palimpsest of history and art. However one particular must be emphasized: though the city has changed its external aspect many times in 25 centuries, its people have remained unchanged. If we wander along Via Tribunali in the space between the Basilicas of S. Lorenzo and S. Paolo Maggiore, we find in the nearby alleys all the characters whom we can imagine populating Naples when it was a Greek city. They have the same way of moving, walking, expressing themselves, of gesticulating, the same physiognomy and bodily characteristics: as it were, a single thread linking together the many differing and discordant historical phases of this city.

Now we pass along the streets of the ancient centre, making our entrance from **Porta Capuana.** This is not the gateway of the decumanus maximus which once opened in the Greek city's walls at the point where the road led to Capua. When the city was extended eastwards, the construction of the new Aragonese city walls necessitated the removal of the gate which was actually closer to Castel Capuano. The present gate was constructed by Giuliano da Maiano in 1484 and is framed between two towers of grey peperino. It is considered one of the jewels of architecture, where all the elements of Florentine artistic tradition may be observed. After passing on the right the 16th century Church of S. Caterina a Formiello, one is faced with the imposing mass of Castel Capuano. Begun in the latter half of the 12th century, it was enlarged by Frederick II of Swabia and adapted as a royal residence. It subsequently underwent a series of alterations among which it is worth recalling that carried out by Pietro da Toledo. In 1540 he transformed it into a seat for the lawcourts, a role which it still fulfills. We now take Via Tribunali, the decumanus maximus, and observe the most important buildings and the elements of lesser architecture or simple buildings which link together the monuments, forming about them, one might say, a choral motif. After Piazzetta Sedil Capuano, over which look the arches of the ancient portico, seat of one of the civic districts, we come to Piazzetta Riario-Sforza. This is dominated by the Dome of the Cathedral and ornamented by the tower of San Gennaro, a votive offering of the citizens, erected by the architect Fanzago in the middle of the 17th century. At the right is the 17th century Monte della Misericordia annexed to which is a church. Among the works of art which this contains is a large canvas

Naples. Porta Capuana

44

by Caravaggio, the Opere di Misericordia. One comes to Via Duomo. The street, one of the cardines of the Greek city, was widened in the last century and is one of the most bustling arteries of the ancient centre. After a climb uphill to the right one comes to a small open space in which stands **the Cathedral,** dedicated to S. Gennaro. The present church was founded at the end of the 13th cent., and has been several times restored and built up to the beginning of this century. It stands on the site of the primitive 5th century Cathedral, which was next to the Basilica of S. Restituta and shared its atrium. The façade was reconstructed in Gothic style at the beginning of the century but preserves the three portals of the original construction. In the central lunette is a Madonna by Tino di Camaino. Inside there are paintings and sculptures by Luca Giordano, Tino di Camaino, Domenico Fontana, Solimena and other artists. **The chapel of S. Gennaro,** on the right, was added as a votive offering by the Neapolitans in the 17th century. It is richly endowed with works of art and has a valuable treasury. Here is preserved the skull of S. Gennaro, together with the ampullae of coagulated blood which becomes liquid twice a year. In the right transept the Minutolo Chapel preserves the original Gothic architec-

Naples, Piazzetta Riario-Sforza

ture and a 13th century mosaic floor. On its wall, 15th century frescoes still recall the style of Pietro Cavallini. Among the sarcophagi of members of the Minutolo family, there is one of Orso by Tino di Camaino. At the far end, under the presbytery, is the Crypt constructed by Cardinal Carafa at the end of the 15th century in elegant Renaissance style. To the left is S. Restituta, the most ancient basilica in Naples, erected in the 4th century and transformed in subsequent ones. From S. Restituta one enters directly into the Baptistry which dates from the second half of the 5th century. We continue up Via Duomo. In Vico Donnaregina stands the 14th century **Church of S. Maria Donnaregina.** It was constructed between 1307 and 1320 by Mary of Hungary, wife of Charles II of Anjou, upon the site of a pre-existing church. The pillars which form the three naves support the Nun's choir, which preserves on its walls frescoes by Pietro Cavallini and assistants. They date from the second decade of the 14th century and form a valuable example of the mural decoration of a Neapolitan Gothic church. In the left wall of the church is the tomb of Mary of Hungary, a work by Tino di Camaino. The remains of the primitive church's flooring are assembled on a panel in a nearby chamber. Return to Via Duomo. Facing the

Naples, Cathedral. The Carafa Chapel

Naples, Church of Donnaregina.
Tomb of Maria of Hungary

Naples, Church of Donnaregina. Floor
(remains)

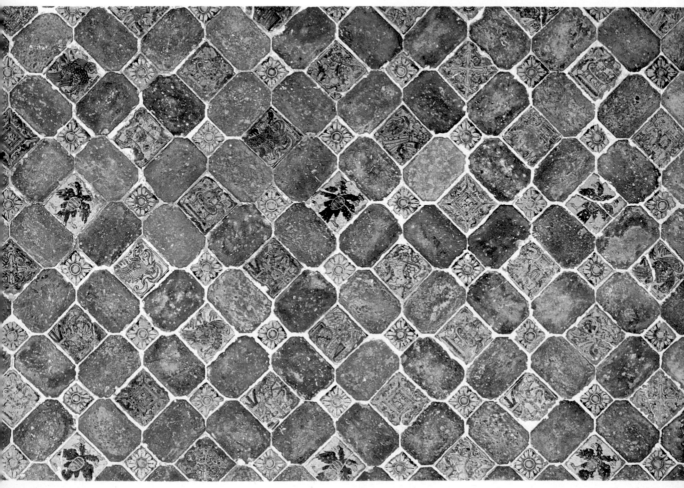

48

Cathedral is situated the convent of the Padri Gerolomini. It was founded by S. Filippo Neri in the 16th century and was enlarged in subsequent centuries. Inside is **the Library,** a grandiose chamber constructed by Guglielmelli in the first half of the 18th century. The finesse and harmony which interlink architectural form, antique furnishings, decorations, frescoes and paintings are noteworthy.

Further ahead is the Piazza S. Gaetano, dominated by the **Church of S. Paolo Maggiore** which stands above a spectacular stairway. It was erected at the end of the 16th century on the ruins of a pre-existing 9th century church, which had, in turn, utilized the site, and a part of the structure of the Temple of the Dioscuri. Two columns remain of the latter. These are inserted in a casual, apparently absurd manner, linked as they are to the late 16th century façade by two pieces of architrave. This can be explained only by a desire and nostalgia for classicism. Naples had always had links to this, notwithstanding the French and Catalan architects who in preceding centuries had brought their native architecture and notwithstanding the traditional Neapolitan receptiveness to any artistic expression from any part of the world. So, S. Paolo Maggiore, in spite of the slight artistic value of

Naples, Monastery of the Gerolomini. Library

the façade, can be considered the symbol of Neapolitan architecture. Returning to the piazza we recall that we are in the ancient Forum. Here were the forensic Basilica and the Curia. Now **the Basilica of S. Lorenzo Maggiore** stands on the site, replacing demolished 6th century church. It was begun in the 13th century and French architects constructed the apse. Later the solemn nave and lateral chapels were completed with the utilisation of ancient columns. In recent years, excavations beneath the present level of the Basilica have revealed the remains of a paleo-Christian church, together with a mosaic pavement. At a still lower level, constructions of the ancient city, among them a section of paved Roman road, are superimposed on an even earlier wall of the Greek epoch. Apart from this stratification of buildings belonging to successive eras, we should recall the tradition which continued for centuries on this spot. The ancient Neapolitans met in the forensic Basilica to elect magistrates or to discuss questions of common interest. Similarly, during the Middle Ages the Neapolitans met in the church and convent of S. Lorenzo, which were constructed on the site of that Basilica. Here they held the general parliaments of the kingdom and discussed matters of a civic nature. The present in-

Naples. Church of S. Paolo Maggiore

terior is rich in paintings and sculpture; works dating from the 14th to the 17th century. The whole is dominated by the magnificent apse.

The yellow tufa of the Neapolitan hills gives off luminous effects and a vibrating golden warmth which change according to the incidence and intensity of the light: effects unknown to the original French Gothic architecture. In the chapels which open off the ambulatory in the apse, we find among other things, the tomb of Catherina of Austria, by Tino di Camaino, and frescoes by the master of S. Ludovico da Tolosa and Robert Oderisi. We return to Piazza S. Gaetano and continue along Via Tribunali. To the left is **the palace of Philip of Anjou.** It preserves its original doorway and the 13th century portico, which is now enlivened by a picturesque market. Go up Via S. Paolo Maggiore again as far as the line of the upper decumanus, or decumanus superior. Here the links with Neapolis are strong. The remains of Greco-Roman constructions, the two arches which straddled the decumanus thus connecting the public baths with the ancient theatre, the very name of the street, Via Anticaglia: all carry us back in time. At the end of Via Armanni stands the Hospital for Incurables. It was founded in 1519 and still preserves some of its original sections, such as the church

Naples, Piazza San Gaetano

Naples,
Church of S. Lorenzo.
Apse

and the sacristy with its furnishings of the period. These are the work of Donato Massa, the same ceramist who, a few years earlier, had completed the majolica cloister of S. Chiara. Return to Via Tribunali by way of Vico Purgatorio. From the curve of the street, we can observe the structure of the Odéon, incorporated in the buildings on the left.

We arrive at S. Maria Maggiore, built in the 17th century by Fanzago above the ruins of one of the four major basilicas of the 6th century. The smallish bell-tower is of the 11th century. Beside the church is the Pontano Chapel, a work of elegant Renaissance architecture which was erected at the end of the 15th century. It was designed, possibly by Fra' Giocondo, for Giovanni Pontano, a famous humanist and secretary to Ferdinand I of Aragon. At the end of Via Tribunali is the Church of S. Pietro a Maiella, erected between the 13th and 14th centuries, and restored to its original form at the end of the last century. In the interior the ceiling paintings by Mattia Preti, dating from mid-17th century and depicting the lives of S. Celestino V and S. Caterina of Alexandria are noteworthy. Now down Via S. Sebastiano as far as the lower decumanus. Today this street changes name several times along its length, but its most common denomination

Naples, Palace of Philip of Anjou. The Small market

is the popular one: **«Spaccanapoli»** (the street which «splits Naples»). When the city was enlarged towards the West in the 16th century, the line of the ancient lower decumanus was extended as far as the hill of S. Martino. So the original length of the street was doubled along a straight line. Consequently, «Spaccanapoli» divides the city quite clearly and distinctly, particularly if one looks down from the belvedere of S. Martino. Some of the most important monuments of the city are aligned along this major street. We will go along only the oldest part, departing from **Piazza Gesù Nuovo.** This piazza was seriously damaged during the last war and in subsequent years. Originally it was separated from the churchyard of S. Chiara by a high wall which surrounded the Franciscan monastery, where later a building was constructed which made a clear separation between the two open spaces. When this building was destroyed, Piazza Gesù Nuovo was almost welded to the churchyard of S. Chiara. Nevertheless no satisfactory architectonic solution was found for the problem of the open space in such an important monumental area. The Church of the Gesù Nuovo was erected at the end of the 16th century, and utilized the façade constructed by Novello di S. Lucano in 1470, for the palace of

Naples. Pontaniana Academy and Bell tower of Pietrasanta

Naples, S. Chiara, Cloister of the Grey Friars. Lello da Roma: The Maestà

the Sanseverinos. In the middle of the piazza is the tower of the Immacolata, a mid-18th century work gaily ornate.

Facing the Gesù Nuovo stands **the convent of S. Chiara.** The buildings of which it consists are vast and complex; the whole is totally closed off by high surrounding walls; the organization is so self-sufficient, both materially and spiritually, that it has been appropriately called «The Franciscan Citadel». The monastery was founded in 1317 by Robert of Anjou and Queen Sancha. It united the buildings necessary for the cloistered life of the Clare sisters. Beside it was a monastery of Grey Friars. The two monasteries were linked and yet separated at the same time in a planning solution which connected one volume to the other, giving major importance to the cloister. Thus, the spiritual centre of the religious community also came to assume primary importance in its architectural expression. The monastery has two cloisters: one for the Clare sisters and one for the Grey Friars. The entrance to the Clares' convent in which is the majolica cloister, lies in the courtyard at the back of the left-hand side of the church. The original fourteenth century arrangement consisted of a colonnade of Gothic arches on pillars. In 1740 Domenico Vaccaro added

Naples. Piazza del Gesù

an ornamentation of incredible elegance. The central space of the cloister is cultivated as a garden and is subdivided by low walls and benches alternating with octagonal pillars. These are adorned with majolicas depicting landscapes and set in cornices, volutes and floral decorations. The majolica ornamentation is by the Neapolitans Giuseppe and Donato Massa. A vine pergola is supported by the pillars, and above the cloister towers the imposing mass of S. Chiara. Between the cloister and the church is situated the Clares' choir. Here, after the bombardment of the 4th August 1943, the fragment of a great fresco came to light. It depicts a Crucifixion and a Pietà and has been attributed to an artist in very close relationship to Giotto. The cloister of the Friars is situated on the right side of the church, but is not easy to visit on account of the cloistral rules. The colonnade, with its low Gothic arches, reveals the influence of Sienese architecture. In the choir a **fresco by Lello da Roma** depicts Christ seated between the Madonna, saints and the donors. The Church of S. Chiara, with its stark severe architecture, is by Gagliardo and Leonardo da Vito and brings to mind the Gothic of Provençal churches. On the sides, slender elegant twin mullioned windows alternate with robust buttresses. On the

Naples, S. Chiara, Convent of the Poor Clares, Majolica Cloister

façade an elegant rose window is inserted in the frame of a pair of towers. The church was restored to its original form after the bombardment of 4th August 1943, and in its vast and solemn interior, we find today reassembled and restored the monuments which were saved from the ruins. Among these are to be noted: the tomb of Robert of Anjou, by Giovanni and Pacio Bertini, at the far end of the presbytery, in the centre: the tomb of Mary of Valois, by Tino di Camaino, on the right wall of the presbytery; also by Tino, the tomb of Charles of Calabria, to the right of the tomb of Robert.

Going along Via S. Chiara as far as Piazza Banchi Nuovi; observe the interesting palace of the 18th century on the corner and, further along **Penna Palace,** in Piazzetta Teodoro Monticelli. It was constructed in 1406 for Antonio Penna, secretary to the king. The ashlars of peperino in the elegant façade are decorated with plumes and Angevin lilies. The low arched portal is framed in a rectangle following a scheme typical of this period. Returning to S. Chiara proceed along «Spaccanapoli». On the left one passes the Filomarino Palace, which preserves in its structure traces of the numerous renovations undergone during the centuries. The portal

Naples, S. Chiara, Convent of the Poor Clares. Majolica Cloister (Detail)

Naples, S. Chiara, Convent of the Poor Clares.
Capitular Hall, Crucifixion

Naples, S. Chiara, Cloister of the Grey Friars
(West side)

is by Sanfelice. In this palace Benedetto Croce lived and died. We reach Piazza S. Domenico Maggiore, dominated at one end by the apse of the **Church of S. Domenico,** which in turn is surmounted by a fine series of palaces. This, too, is one of that group of Gothic churches constructed by the Angevins at the end of the 13th and during the 14th century. Attached to this church was the convent which the Dominicans transformed into a centre of study and culture. Here Thomas Aquinas taught theology. The church was altered several times in successive centuries and has lost its original 14th century appearance, but it still retains the fine Gothic doorway and the wooden door. Inside is the 13th century Crucifix which spoke to St. Thomas Aquinas. Apart from works by Roberto Oderisi, Colantonio, Tino di Camaino and Mattia Preti, we find an Annunciation by Titian. The tomb of Vittoria Colonna is also to be found in S. Domenico.

Piazza S. Domenico Maggiore, Piazzetta del Nilo, Largo Corpo di Napoli: three squares which are interlinked in a series of differently proportioned, but intimately related areas; each environment participating in the life of the other. Here was the Alexandrian quarter in Greek Naples. The traffickings, the comings and goings and confusion can have been no less

Naples. Largo Corpo di Napoli

Naples,
Church of S. Angelo a Nilo.
Donatello:
Tomb of Cardinal Brancaccio

than they are today. The ancient statue of the River Nile, venerated by the Alexandrians, is still to be found there in Largo Corpo di Napoli. It was probably also in this area that the Temple of Isis stood. To the right is the Church of S. Angelo a Nilo. It contains **the tomb of Cardinal Brancaccio,** constructed between 1426—28 by **Donatello** and assistants. Here Donatello, on a tomb which still maintains the Gothic style, has created a low-relief of the Assumption possessing all the elements characteristic of the renaissance of the arts at this time. Continuing along Via S. Biagio dei Librai, to the left is Santangelo Palace, erected by Diomede Carafa in the middle of the 15th century. It is one of the most interesting Renaissance buildings containing elements of Florentine architecture mixed with others of Catalan derivation. Further along, in Via S. Gregorio Armeno are the church and convent of the same name. They stand on the site of the Temple of Ceres. The church was reconstructed in 1580. The baroque decoration of the interior is extremely rich. In Via S. Gregorio Armeno there are numerous shops of the « f i g u r a r i », artisans who make the figures for cribs. The street acquires a special fascination during the Christmas festivities when the shops overflow with these figures.

Naples. Church of S. Gregorio Armeno

THE BAY

The different elements which make up the Bay of Naples give it a character of unity. Each element — natural landscape, human settlements and vestiges of antiquity — bears a close relationship to the others. Naples, Vesuvius, the islands, the houses and villages of the coast, the remains of unearthed cities, the sea itself, share a unique environment defined by one word which epitomizes and expresses all: the Bay. For this reason, a knowledge of the city of Naples is only complete when integrated with a knowledge of the various places which share in the life of the Bay. **Vesuvius** is an important element in the Neapolitan landscape. It is characterized in unmistakable fashion by its profile. The clearcut contours of this barren mass have come to take part in every representation of Naples. It is regarded affectionately by the Neapolitans: they dedicate songs to it — such as «Funiculì, funiculà», and hand down legends — such as that of the origin of the wine Lacryma Christi.

An excursion as far as the crater of Vesuvius constitutes an unforgettable experience. The fertile lower slopes, rich in vineyards, are succeeded by scenery which becomes ever more bare and barren, until at the peak it is desolate and terrifying. As one climbs, marvellous panoramas gradually open up over the Bay. The mountain itself creates within us a particular mood by its great solitude and silence, by the sense of the infinite and eternal. This is an impression which Leopardi was able to experience and he expressed it poetically in his lyric poem «La Ginestra» (The Gorse Plant).

The eruption of Vesuvius in A.D. 79 destroyed **Pompeii and Herculaneum.** However, buried and protected by ash or mud, the elements which made up the face of each city have been preserved almost intact up to the present day: buildings and streets, works of art and simple furnishings. So their re-discovery allows us to reconstruct today an environment, a way of life, an entire civilization. Generally only fragments of ancient cities survive for us. The ruins scattered about in archaeological regions, or incorporated into later buildings are always the remains of public edifices: temples, theatres, baths. That is to say, they represent only the formal aspect of social life in classical antiquity. Therefore the testimony offered by these two cities is all the more precious. The shops with their equipment, the dwellings with their furnishings and utensils still intact, the streets with graffiti on the walls: these are the things which give us a glimpse of every aspect of the life and daily routine of a population. It is through the homes in particular that we reconstruct an image of the society of the time. The climate made it possible to attain that light and warmth which every human needs. Undoubtedly this was an important factor in determining the nature of the home and its architecture. The dwelling is closed on the outside by high walls and on the inside revolves around various open spaces. These, namely the atrium, peristyle, garden and exedra, are enlivened by vegetation, and the colours of plants and flowers are often represented on the painted walls of the rooms. The need for light and greenery, add to this a desire to enjoy the panorama over the Bay. Accordingly, whenever it is possible, the house opens on the outside into loggias sheltered by pergolas. Opening off are small rooms for relaxation, viewpoints from which to enjoy the scenery of land and sea. This particular aspect of the house determined the character and appearance of the city. It has remained during the centuries, the unchanged expression of the culture and tradition of a people who have developed from this landscape. Not only does it characterize the houses unearthed in Herculaneum and Pompeii, but it is still a telling element in the traditional house of the coastal villages. But there are numerous indications of an architectural tradition linked to the setting, the landscape and the way of life. One of these is the persistent fashion of **the suburban villa.** Is there not possibly one single thread connecting the luxurious villas of antiquity, rising beyond the city gates, with those equally elegant villas which flourished in the same Vesuvian landscape during the 18th century? The Villa of Diomedes, the Villa of Mysteries, the Villa of Papyruses, la Favorita, Villa Campolieto, Villa Pignatelli, with their parks and gardens, their columned arcades facing the sea, their fountains and nympheums: all are an expression of a unique culture, a unique sensitivity for Nature and scenery which has been handed down

Pompeii, Vico Storto (The Crooked Lane)

through the centuries. Yet another indication: the continuing architectural and decorative tradition appears in the cloister of the Clare sisters which we saw in the ancient centre of Naples. The pergola resting on pillars adorned with majolica belongs to the same taste which had produced at Pompeii, seven hundred years previously, gardens such as that of the «Villa with Mosaic Columns».

The environmental unity of the Gulf does not suffer when the mountainous profile of the Monti Lattari and the **Sorrento Peninsula** take over from the linear design of the Vesuvian landscape. Here the natural environment is of rich contrasts: it is broken along the coast into rocky promontories, small inlets and rocks jutting out over the sea. Higher up, the profile of the hills becomes gentler and the vegetation is extremely rich in vines and citrus groves. The houses, which are clustered in villages and small towns along the coast, at a higher level are scattered over the country-side. Architecturally speaking, the house follows the traditional scheme of the Italian house, of which we have seen so many examples in the excavated towns. Its external openings are few and small, internally it opens into gardens. Often it is surmounted by terraces, with pergolas sup-

Herculaneum

ported by simple white plastered columns. The vaulted roofing over single rooms is visible from the outside (extrados vaults) and provides a utilization of space which frequently results in formal values of great interest. In the urban areas there are examples of 18th century architecture, mainly churches with the cusps of the bell-towers decorated in coloured majolicas. This is a typical element of these places but clearly of oriental derivation. The main road winds along the coast, through the small towns and touching the Bay in numerous panoramic spots. But it is a real delight to go discovering the Sorrento Peninsula along the numerous back roads which climb the slopes. Sometimes they make their way between high tufa walls over which hang citrus groves. Sometimes they reach the peak of some hill from which it is possible to see, together yet divided, the Bays of Salerno and Naples. The citrus grove provides a landscape characteristic of the Peninsula and it is interesting to see how it changes during the seasons. In winter, mats are put on special supports to protect the lemons and oranges from frosts. In summer they are heaped on the same supports in a way which makes them look like small cases suspended above the trees. The landscape thereby acquires its own special and unmistakeable

Sorronto

appearance. **Sorrento** and the nearby towns gradually diminish in life and activity as one approaches the extreme limit of the Peninsula.

One feels shut off from time travelling along the narrow roads around the headland of the Campanella. It is a landscape of solitude. That sea and those rocks remind us of the legend of the Sirens and finally we realize its significance. Capri is near, facing us, and we can distinguish all its details. To speak of **Capri** is difficult. Its shores, its rocks, its caves are too celebrated, the ruins of the Roman villas and the traditional aspects are too famous. There is nothing which one can say, unless in paraphrase of other writings. Therefore we leave it to the tourist to seek and find the natural sights, the typical urban landscape, the remains of classical antiquity. We propose instead, an unusual Capri itinerary which is full of surprises: the discovery of a few very old churches. They bear witness to an artistic tradition which has left at Capri, as all over southern Italy, records of great interest, not only for scholars, but also for the visitor, who finds them in a highly evocative natural setting. The first of these churches is S. Costanzo at Marina Grande. It dates back to the 10th century and, notwithstanding some 14th century additions, preserves all the characteristics

Sorrento Coastline. Sant'Agnello

of Byzantine architecture. This is particularly clear in the arching system of the cupola, in the plan, originally a Greek cross, and in the entire spatial layout. The columns supporting the cupola are today poor specimens, replacing the four splendid examples in porphyry which came from Roman villas and were removed in the 18th century. In the small Church of S. Maria delle Grazie, also probably of the 10th century, we are confronted with a three-naved basilican plan. This church rises in the centre of Capri, in Via Fuorlovado, among a labyrinth of streets where the traditional Capri architecture seems full of life. From the outside there is no suggestion of the great interest this church offers, but upon entering one is struck by the unusual architecture. The three naves are divided by the shafts of columns and beautiful capitals which came from some building of the Roman era. In the right apse, a fresco depicting the Virgin and Child between two saints belongs to that Neapolitan school which was influenced by the style of Sienese artists. Leaving the inhabited area of Capri, one walks towards Monte San Michele, where, in ancient times, there stood a Roman building, perhaps an imperial palace.

There remains a series of cisterns. One of these cisterns covered by

Capri, Villa Jovis

barrel vaulting was turned into a Church dedicated to S. Michael the Arch-angel during the early Middle Age. Today almost nothing remains of the chapel, which is no longer used for religious purposes. There is only the chamber with its Roman vault and the hint of a ruined apse upon which we still find figures of saints; beautiful frescoes of the 11th century, superimposed upon two layers of earlier paintings, which proves that the cistern was transformed into a church as far back as the early Middle Ages. As we descend from Monte S. Michele we find a small church. After the chapel we have just seen was suppressed, this church took its name. It too preserves oriental characteristics in its extrados cupolas and its win-dows, so arranged as to give the interior that unreal diffused light which is so typical of Byzantine architecture. This possibly dates from a little later than San Costanzo. Last of all, S. Maria Cetrella, clinging to the side of Monte Solaro in an assembly of masses which one might term casual. The Bay is closed to the North-West by a complex of islands and promon-tories, which together create a scene of incredible fascination. The most extraordinary discoveries can be made sailing among the rocks, inlets and promontories, in the craters of volcanoes transformed into tiny harbours

Cumae. Cavern of the Sibyls

Cumae

below the cliffs of yellow tufa. **Nisida,** the Cape and port of **Misenum, Baiae,** the Acropolis of **Cumae,** the rocks of **Procida,** the **Castle of Ischia** and the lakes: all are part of a natural landscape which assumes ever new and different aspects when observed from the sea. In spite of human settlements, which in some parts have altered the natural configuration of the Bay, this part exercises a subtle fascination, a nostalgic recall to the facts of history and the legends of these places and to poetry which they inspired. The Sibyl of Cumae, her meeting with Aeneas and the prophecy scene — dramatically recounted episodes of Vergil's Aeneid which are set in that cave of Cumae where brilliant rays of light are cast upon the geometrically cut walls in the tufa. **Cumae,** the most ancient city of the bay, is still today the most fascinating. Its Acropolis, dense with oaks, overlooks the plain and the sea. It was founded by the Greeks and remained for centuries the centre and cradle of Hellenism in Campania, its bulwark against Etruscans and Samnites. There is much significance in the appearance of a paleo-Christian basilica, constructed on the peak of the Acropolis over the Temple of Jupiter. The ruins of both today are confused and mingled: the continuity of a tradition and, more boldly expressed, a «creed», appear evident in the architectural resolution which placed the presbytery of the Christian basilica in the sanctuary of the pagan temple, preserving and respecting its architecture, its niched walls and possibly its decoration. Near Cumae the lake of Avernus, also connected with the legend of Aeneas, reflects its green-clad shores in mysterious leaden waters. Historical events and a fortunate combination of political and commercial happenings made **Pozzuoli** one of the most important ports of the Mediterranean. It maintained uncontested for centuries its role as a link between Rome and the Orient. The richness of its one-time buildings is evidence of the prosperity and well-being which this role brought to the city. Grandiose remains exist of a theatre, two amphitheatres, a circus, temples, baths and thermal spas. The complex of harbour works has been lost due to the phenomenon of bradyseism and the super-imposing of more recent constructions. Only documents, representations of the topography of the ancient city, testify to the vastness of the port and the importance of its maritime trade. This corner of the Bay is animated by the lively commercial and maritime market. Next in the landscape, after the interval of the Lucrine lake, comes the calm peaceful inlet of **Baiae.** The imperial villas, the palace of the

Pozzuoli. Temple of Serapis

Caesars on the promontory where the castle now stands, the sumptuous villas of the Roman patricians scattered over the hills and along the coast, the baths with their colonnades, loggias and exedrae: of all these, grandiose ruins remain which testify to the Romans' predilection for Baiae. Further along, **Misenum** completes the Peninsula with further important evidence: the military port developed first under the control of Cumae and was subsequently transformed by the Romans into a naval base of prime importance. Thus, in the arc of the Bay of Pozzuoli, we discover three points which allow us to evaluate the importance and prestige of this land; three most interesting categories under which to study the life and society of the time: Pozzuoli and its commercial port, a fundamental base for the conquest of the markets of the Orient; Baiae, the highly refined holiday place for emperors and the best known figures of Roman society; Misenum, whose naval harbour, base of the Romans' Tyrrhenian fleet, defended the prestige of Rome by sea, in association with the Adriatic naval base of Ravenna. The promontories of the Bay of Pozzuoli are extended into the sea by two islands, **Procida** and **Ischia.** The two islands, which so closely resemble each other in their natural landscape, are characterized in their towns by

Procida

picturesque groups of brightly coloured houses clustered along the slopes or on the shore. In Ischia the situation of the castle is in contrast with the traditional type of building. The village is spread over a small island connected to the mainland by a bridge. It consists of buildings of various epochs, closed within a circle of walls that descend almost to the sea. From the 1500's to the 1800's the D'Avalos were lords of the place. The family combined the warlike virtues of its men with the literary talents of its women: Costanza, sister of Innico, Maria of Aragon, wife of Alfonso, and Vittoria Colonna, wife of Ferrante.

The port of Ischia is a one-time volcanic crater. Here the design of the natural landscape is underlined by the fishermen's houses along the shore and happily inserted between cliffs and promontories (in the indigineous vegetation where the Italian pine predominates). Even going around hurriedly it is easy to get an idea of the features of the island, from the solitary inlets to the rural scenery of Monte Epomeo, from the cool, rich pine-groves to the burning sands of the thermal areas, from the remains of ancient civilization collected in the museum beneath the Sanctuary of S. Restituta at Lacco Ameno to the simple fishermen's houses.

Ischia. The Aragonese Castle

INDEX

CORSO VITTORIO EMANUELE II   CASTEL NUOVO   RIVIERA DI CHIAIA

PALAZZO REALE   VILLA COMUNALE